Dance Lovers
Coloring Book

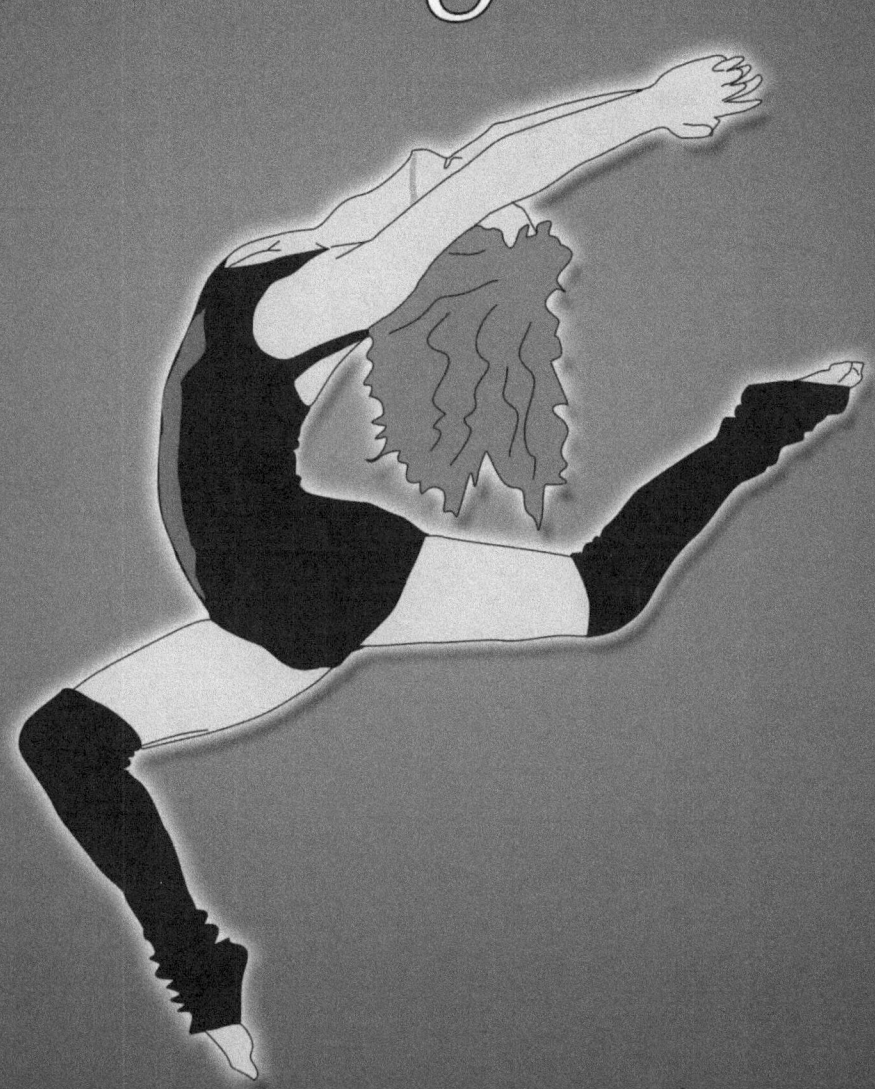

Jasmine Taylor

ISBN 978-0-359-51822-7

9 780359 518227

90000

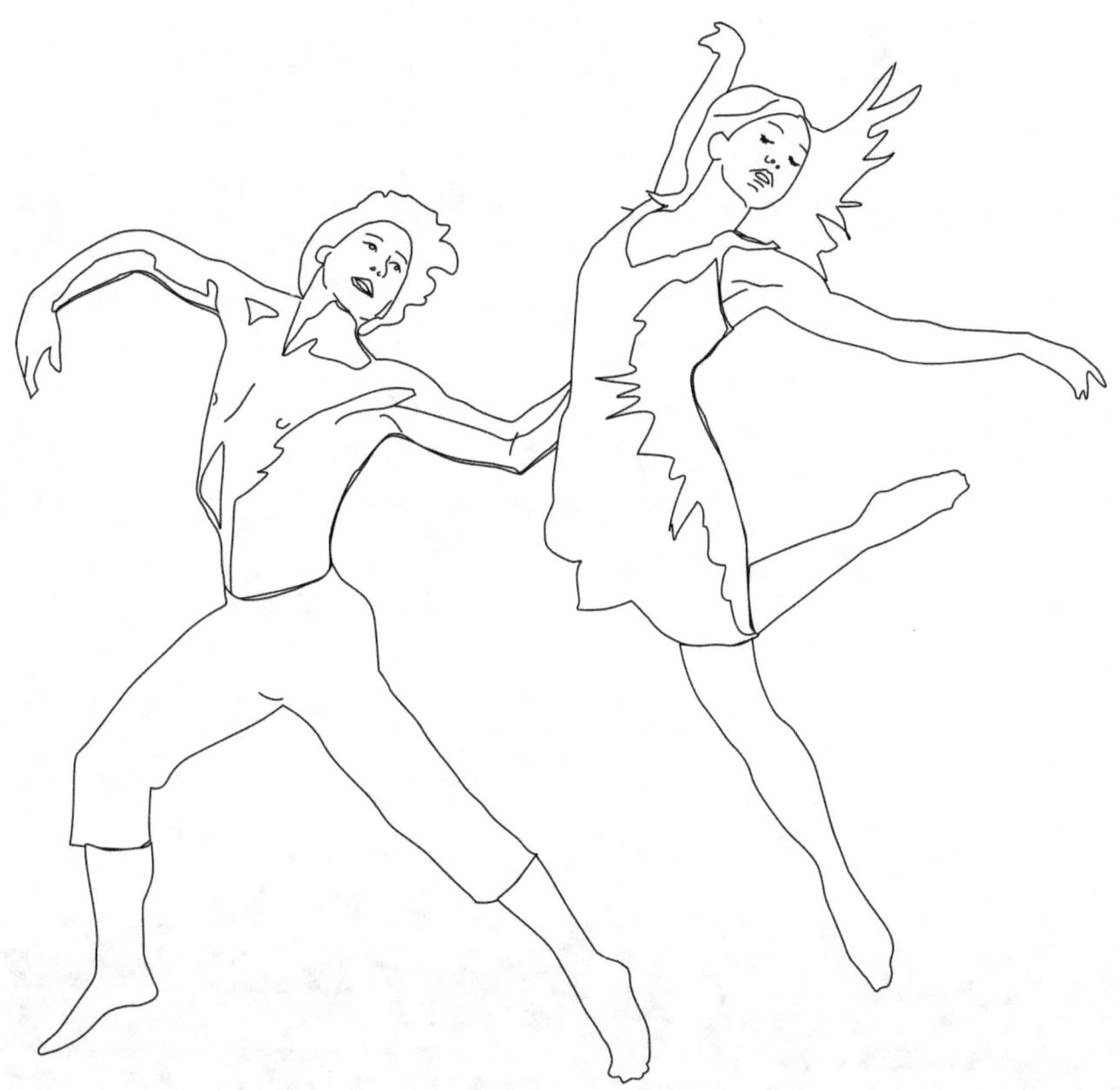

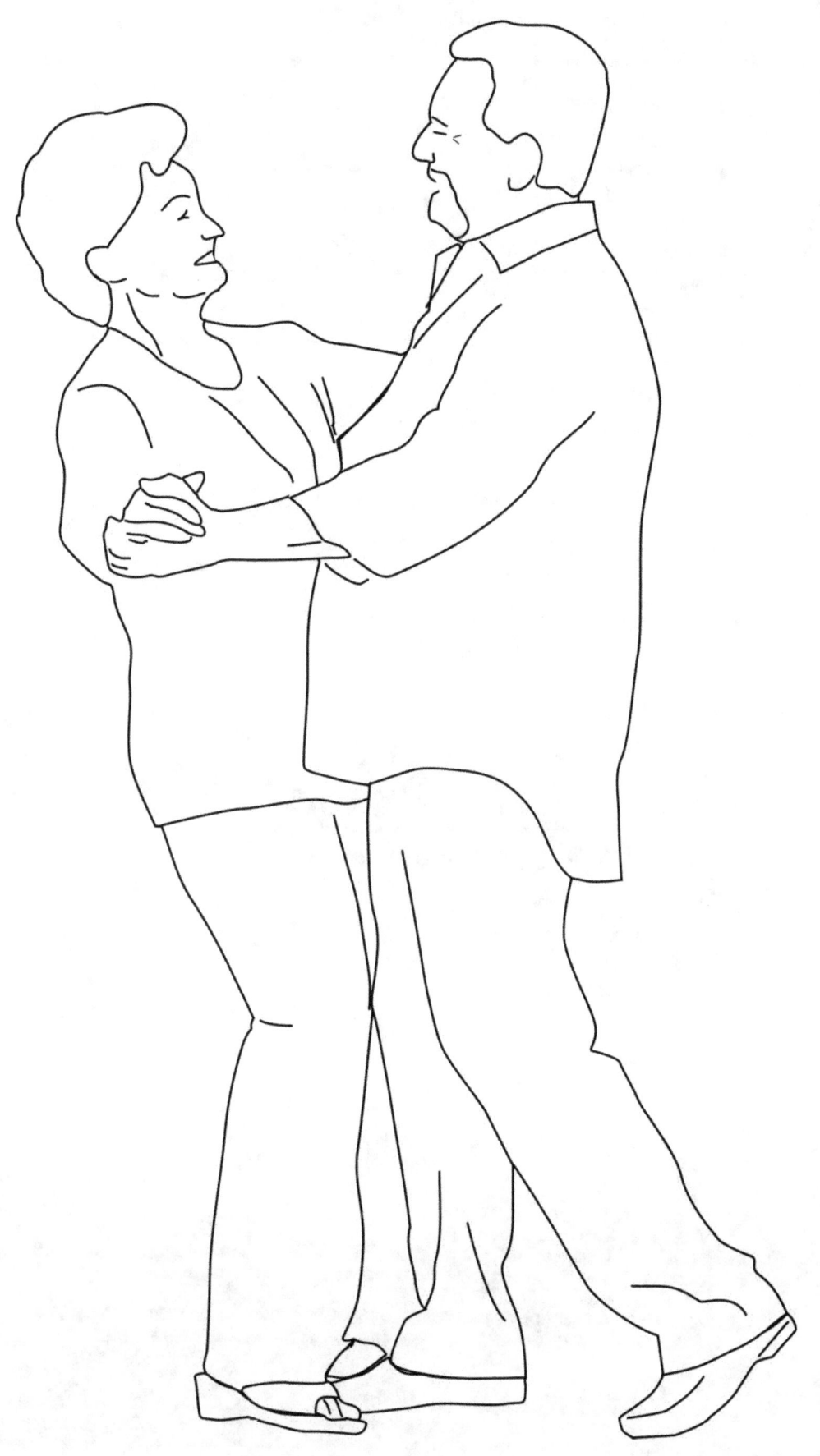

ARTIST

_____

NAME

_____

DATE

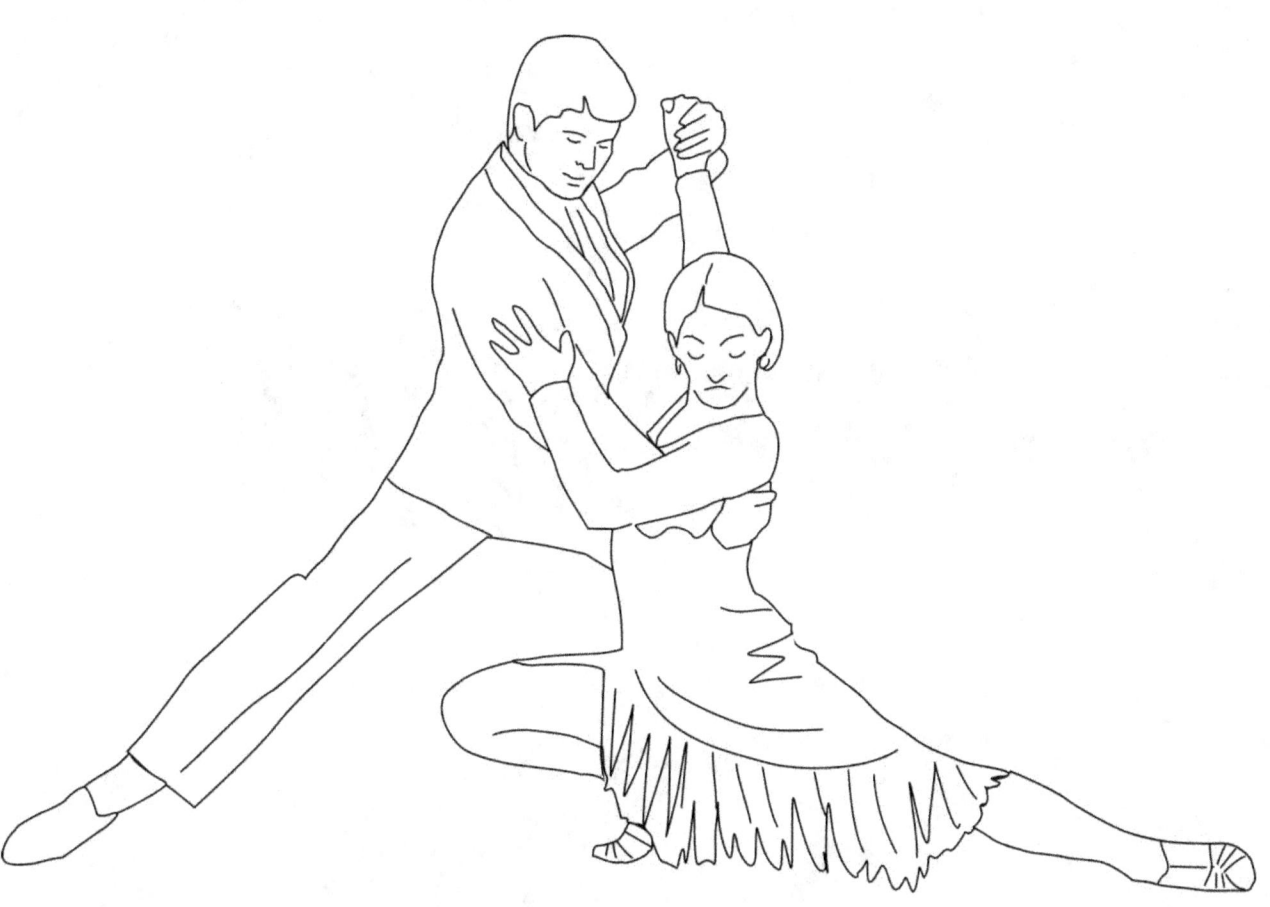

ARTIST

_____

NAME

_____

DATE

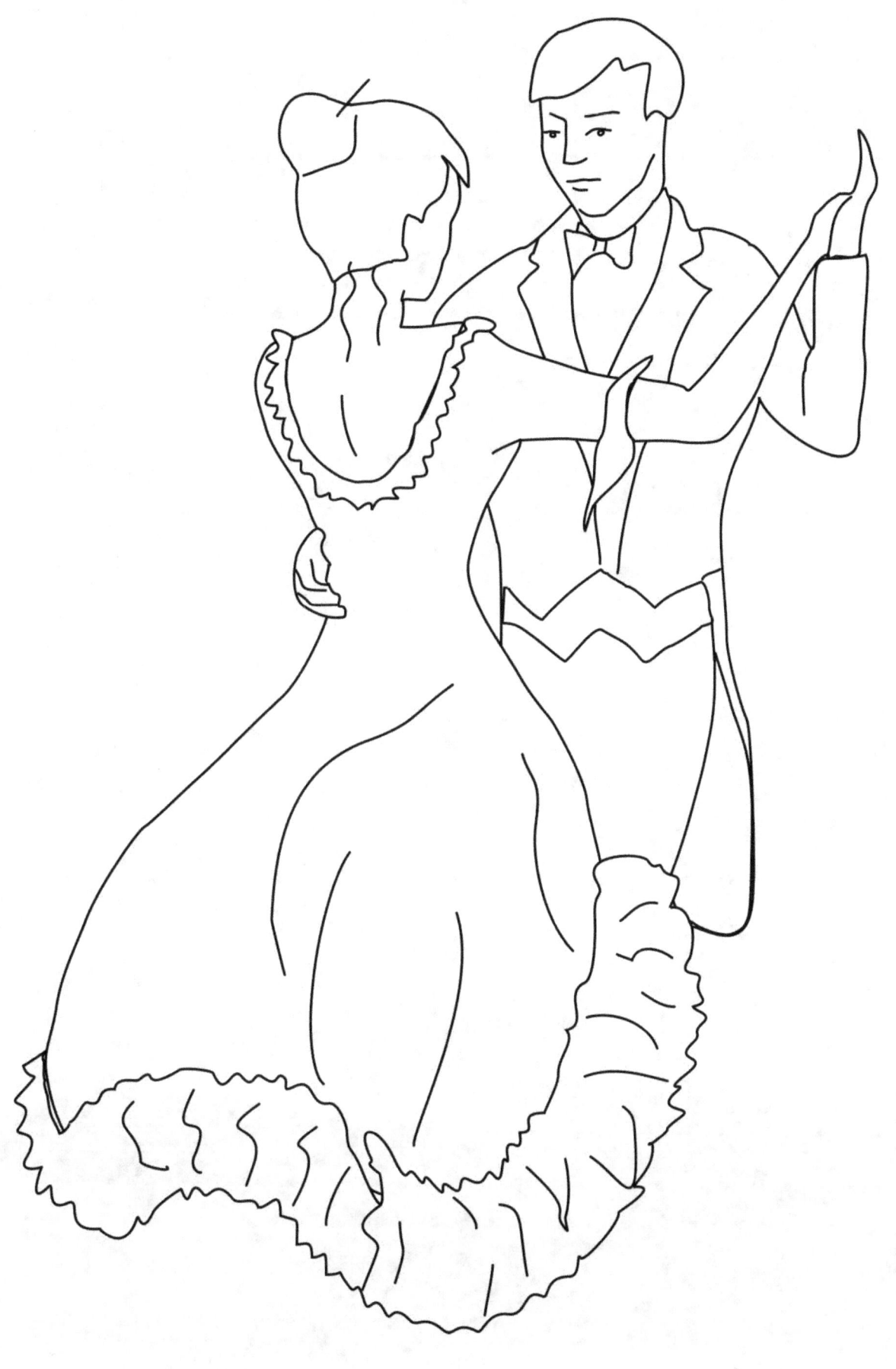

_____
NAME

_____
DATE

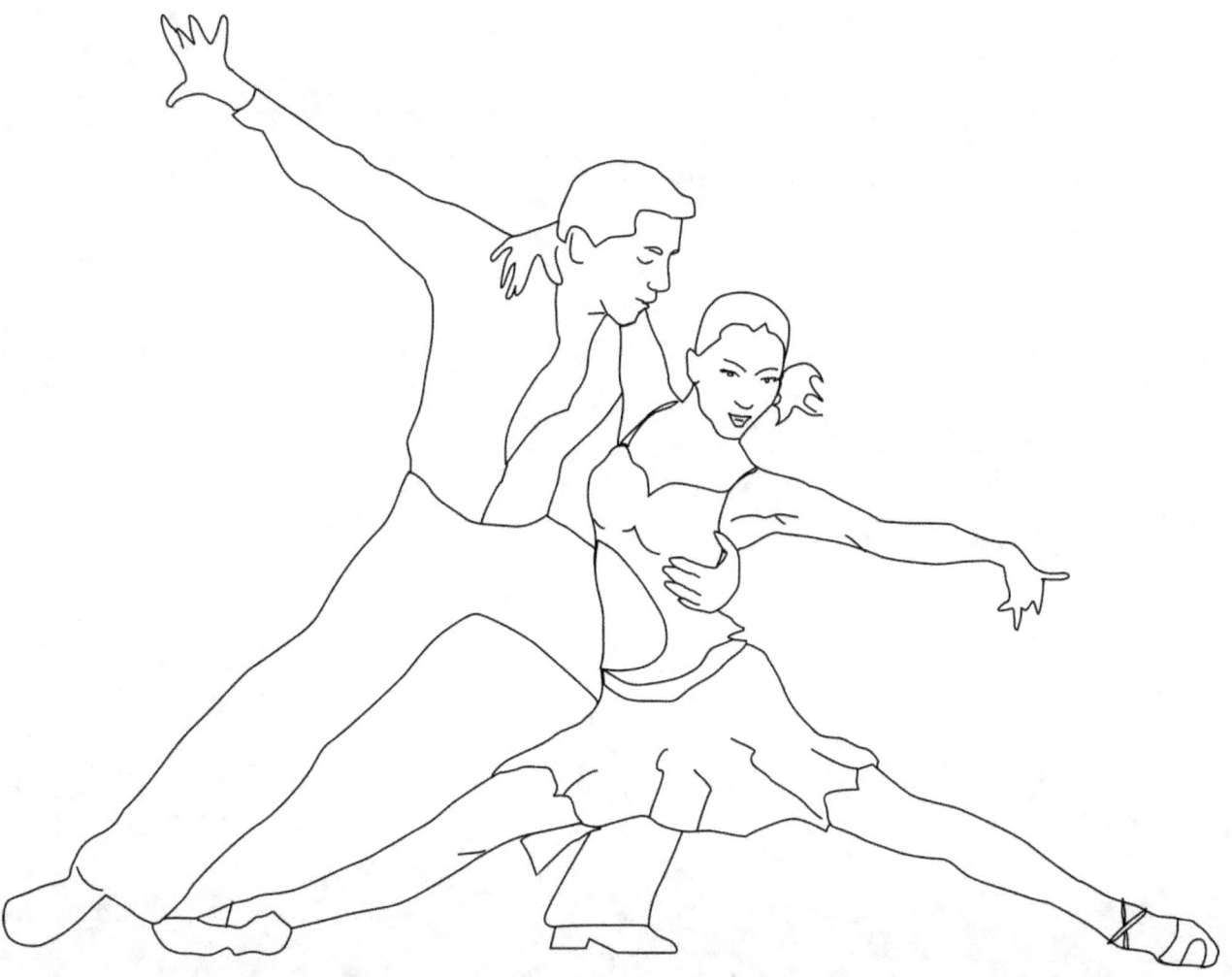

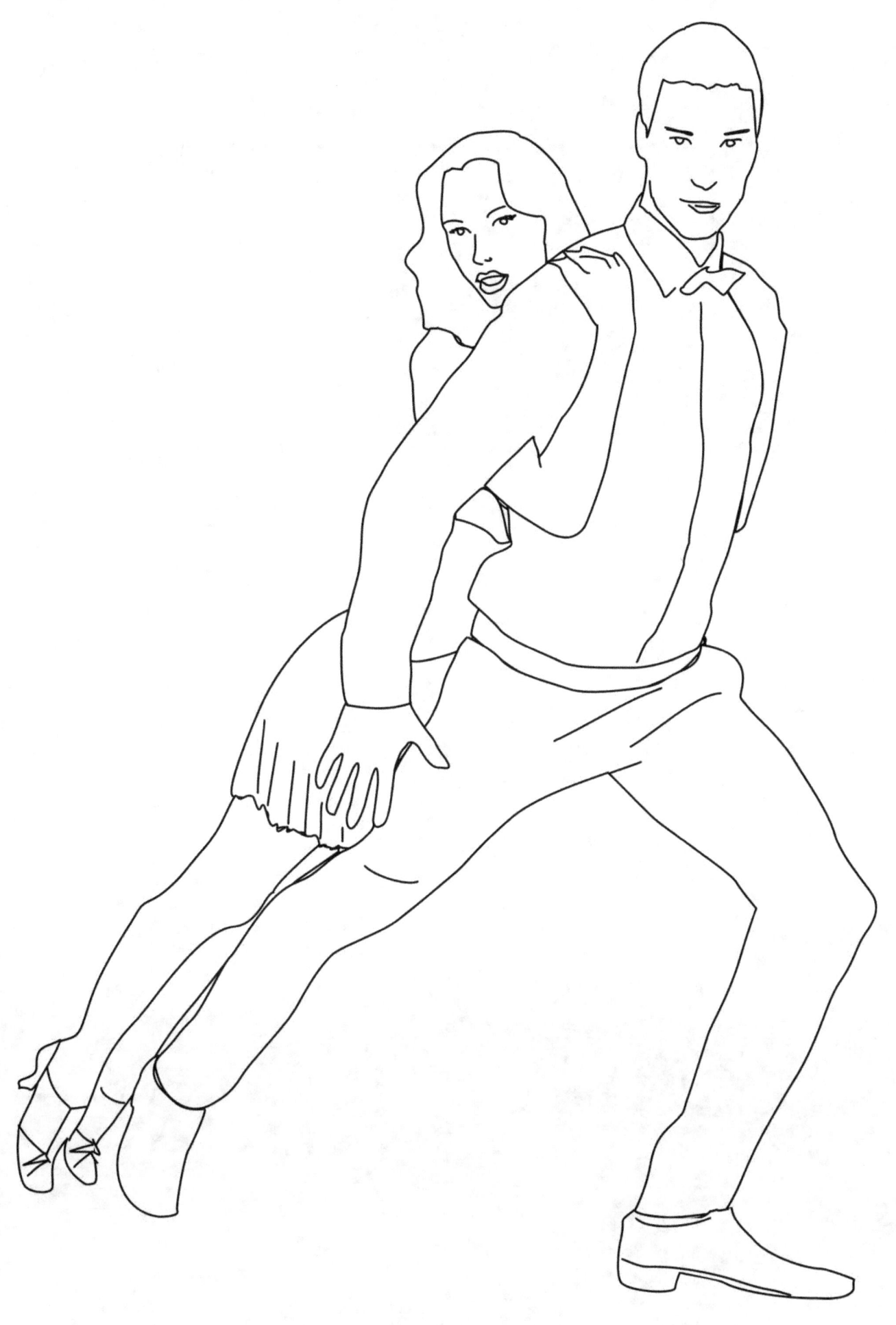

_____
NAME

_____
DATE

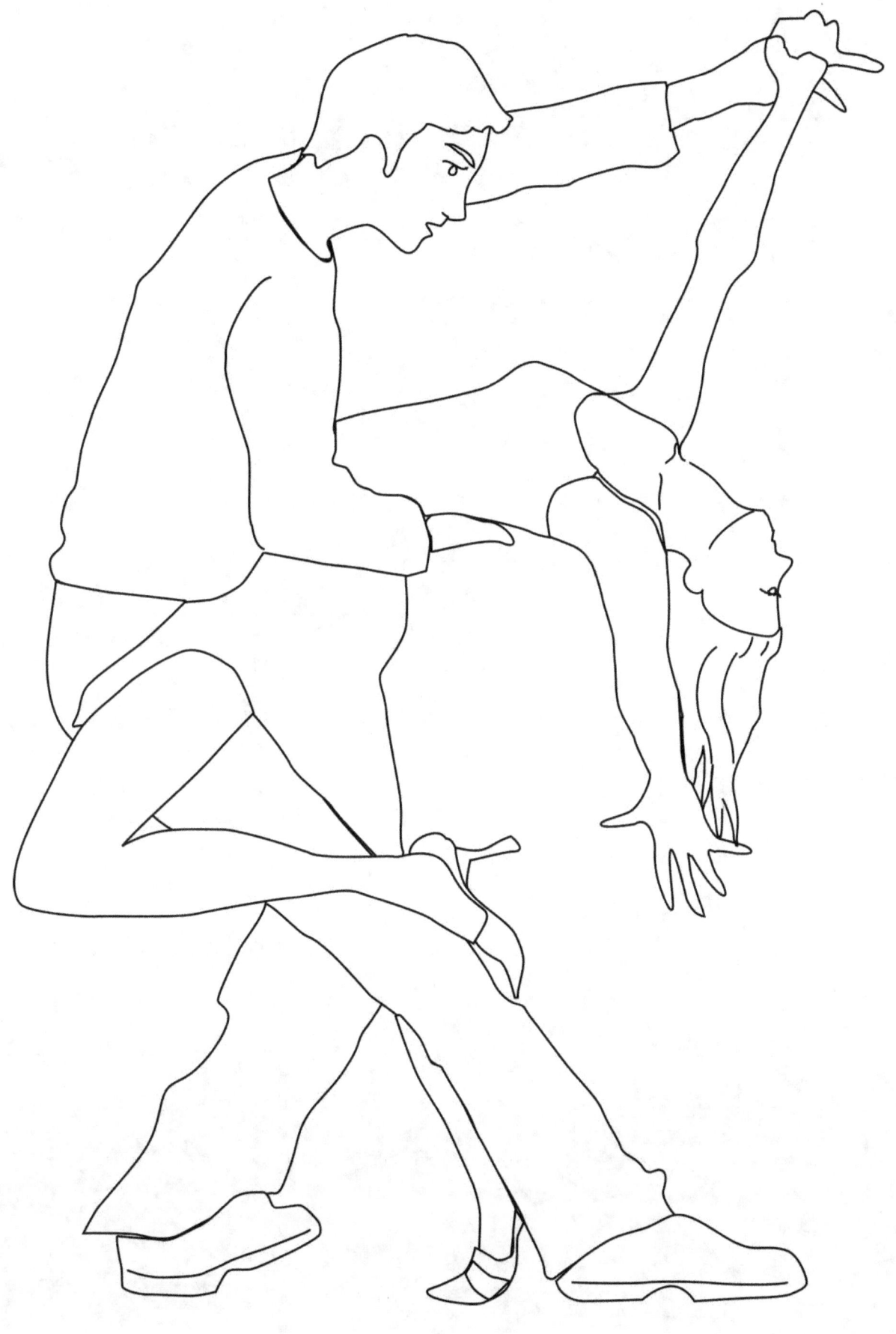

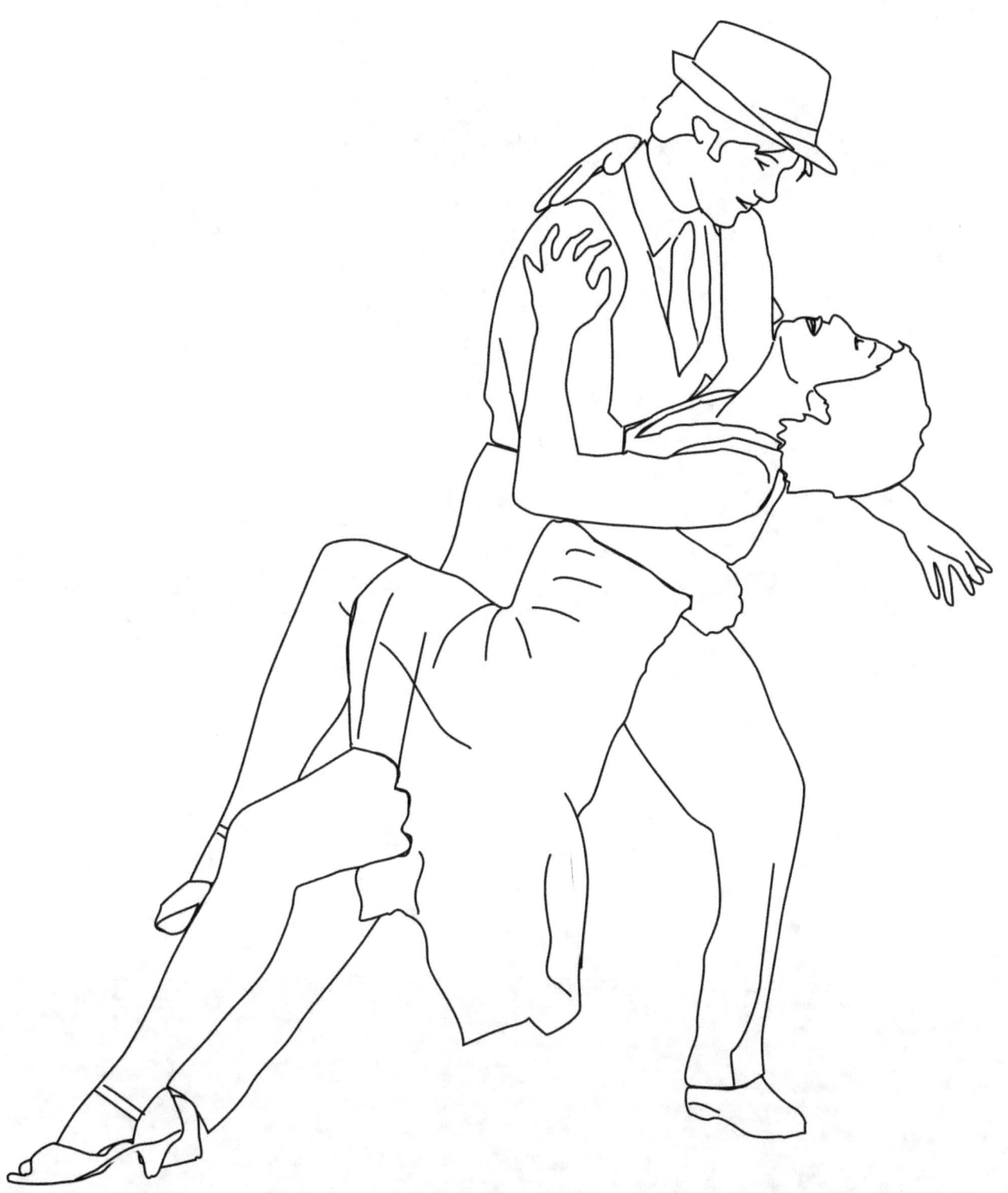

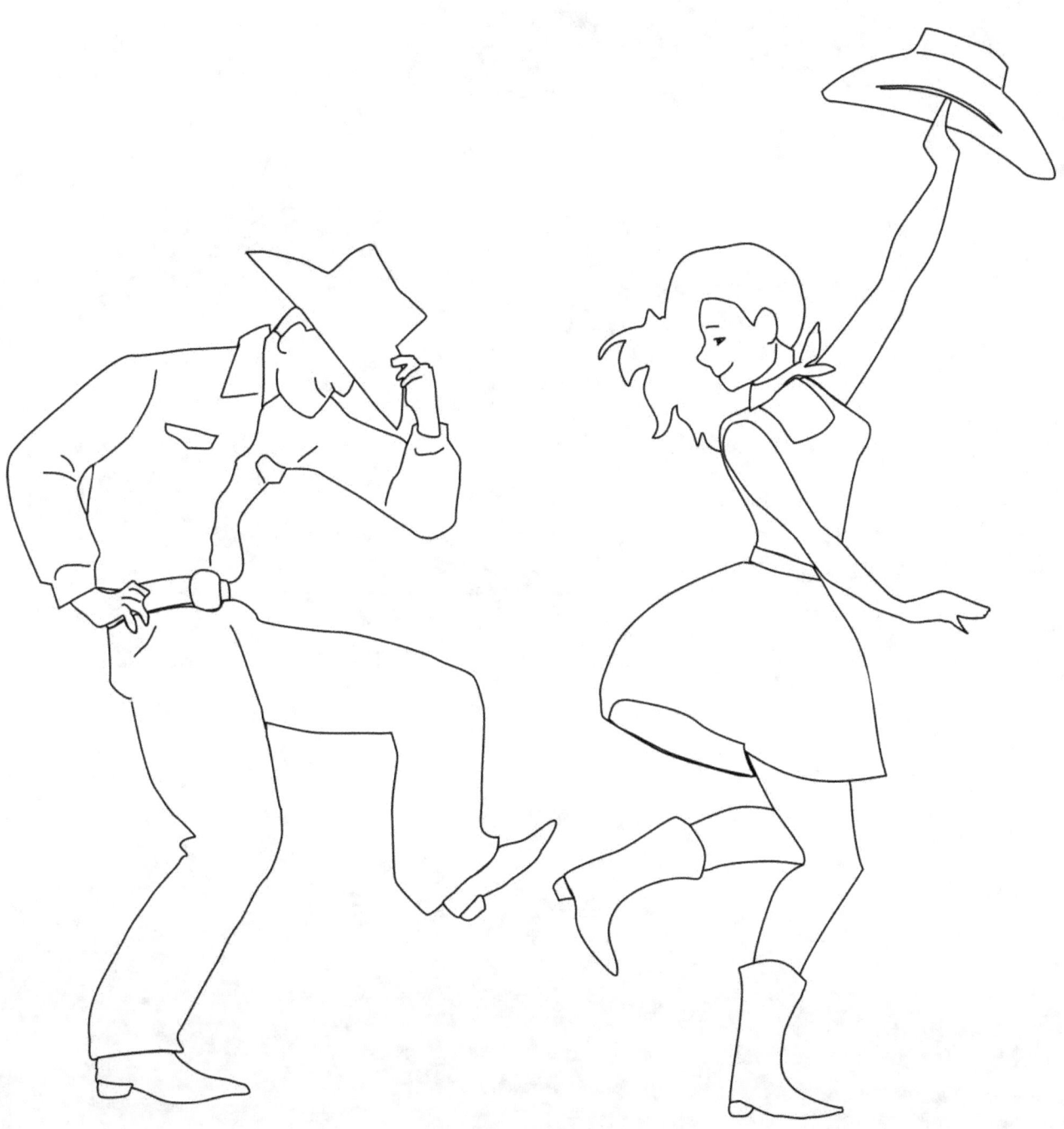

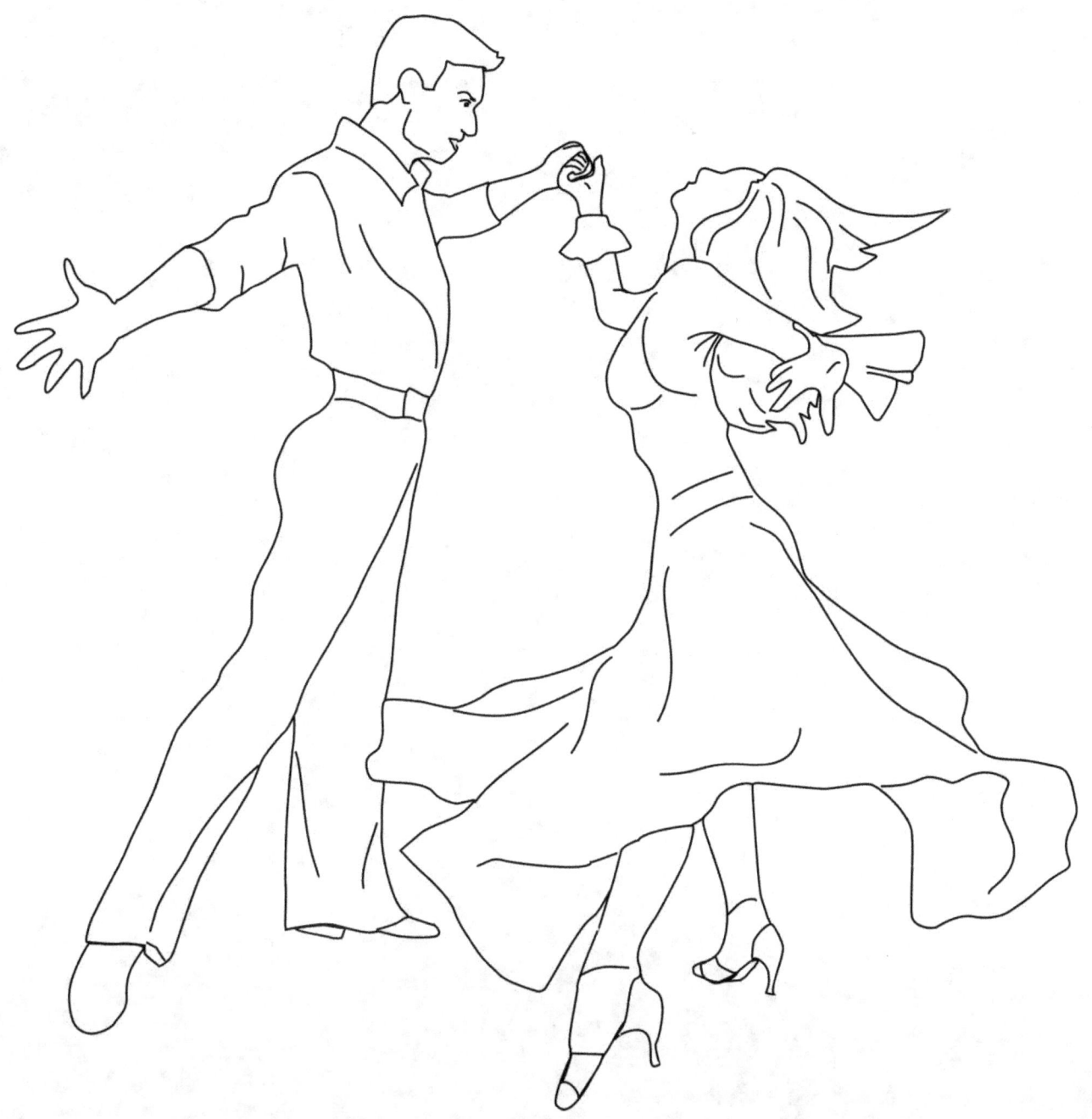

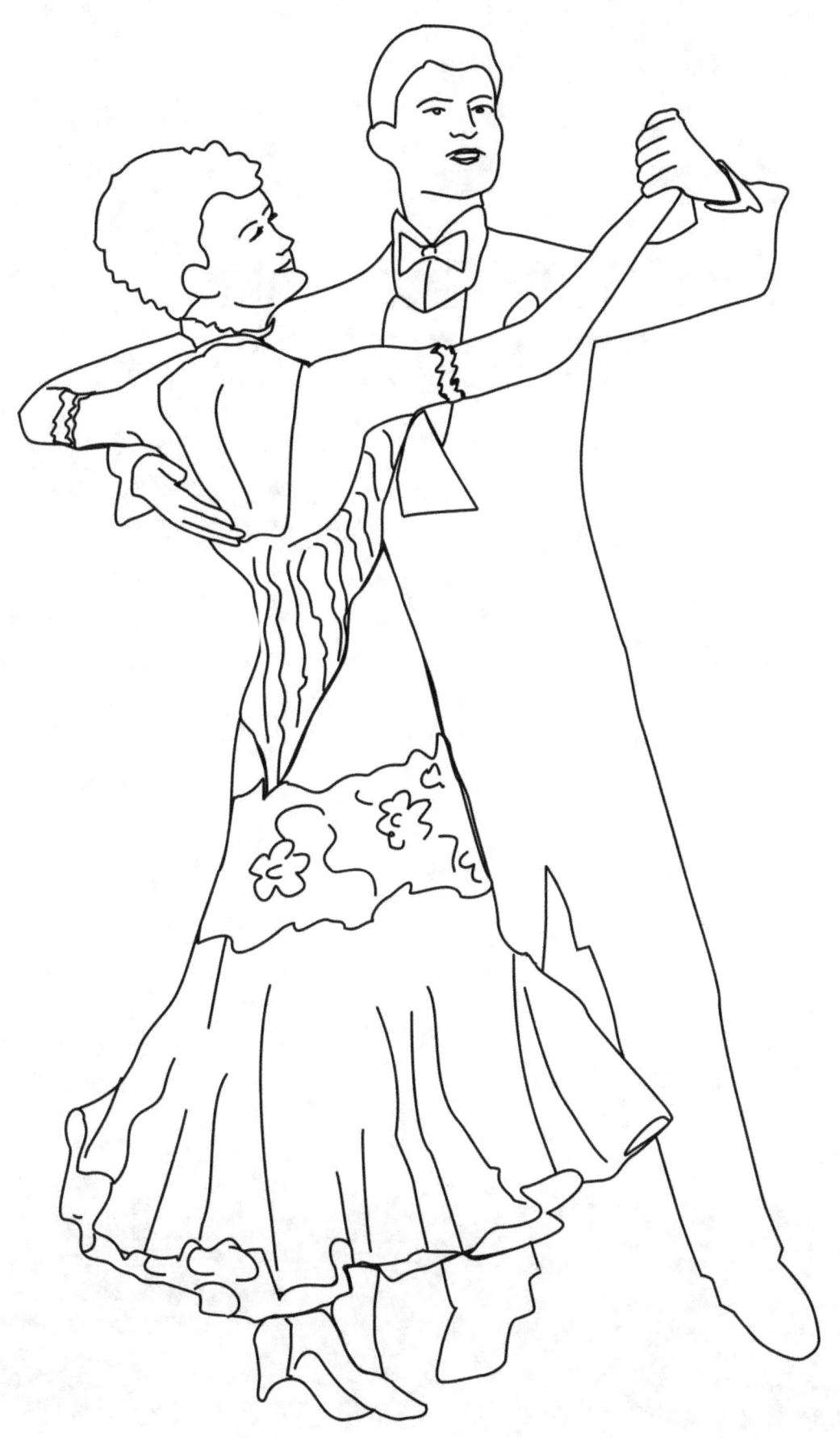

NAME

DATE

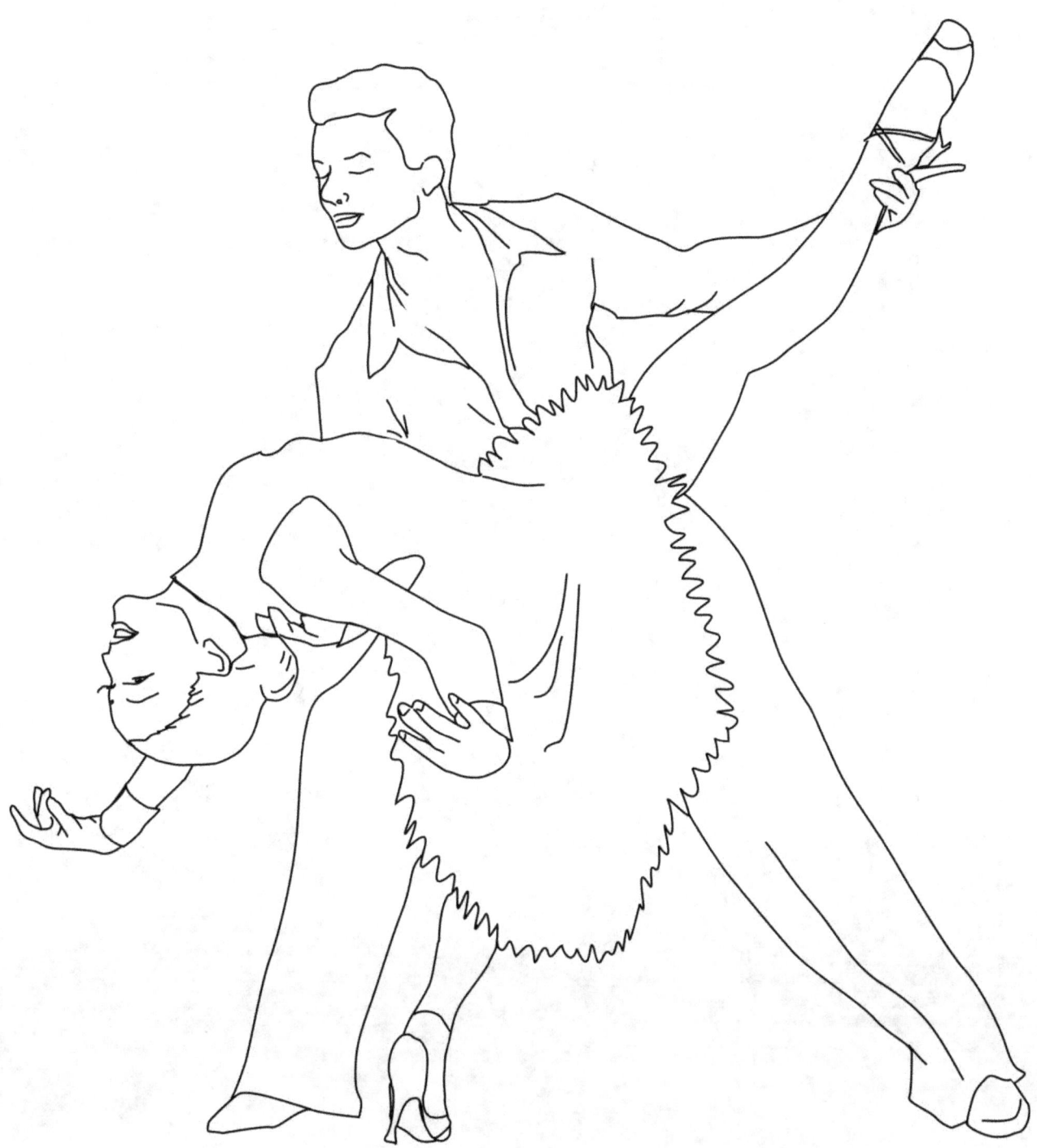

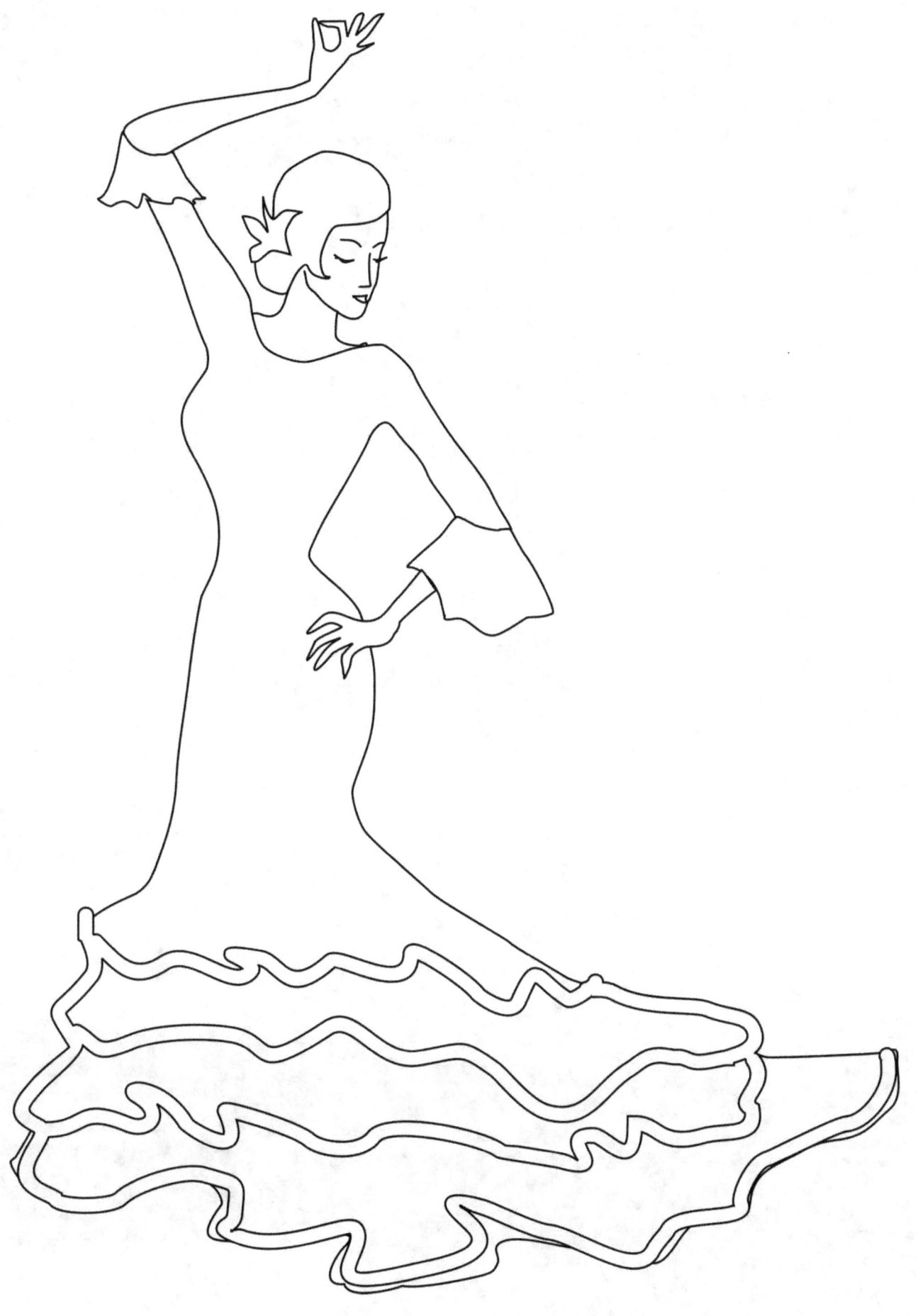

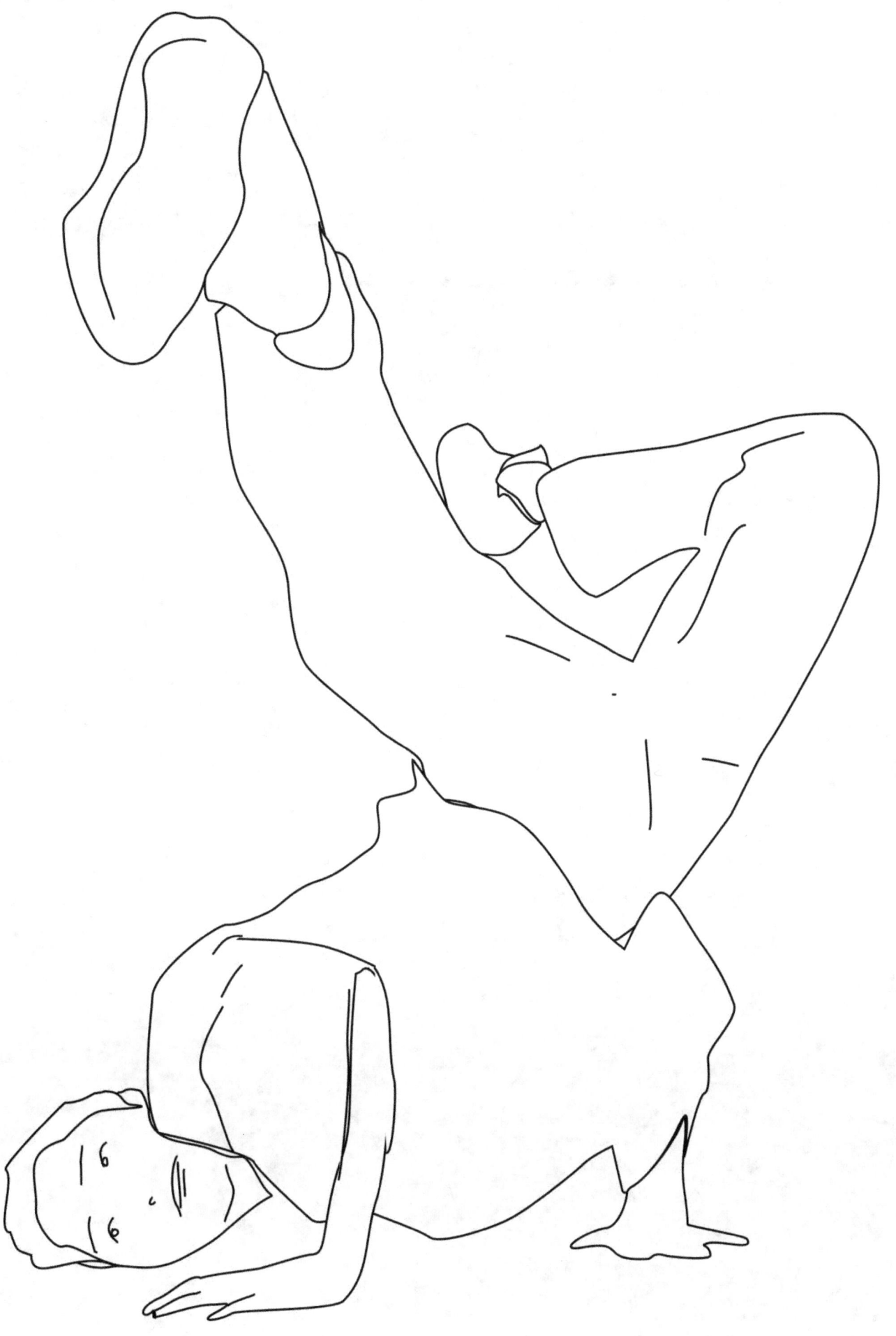

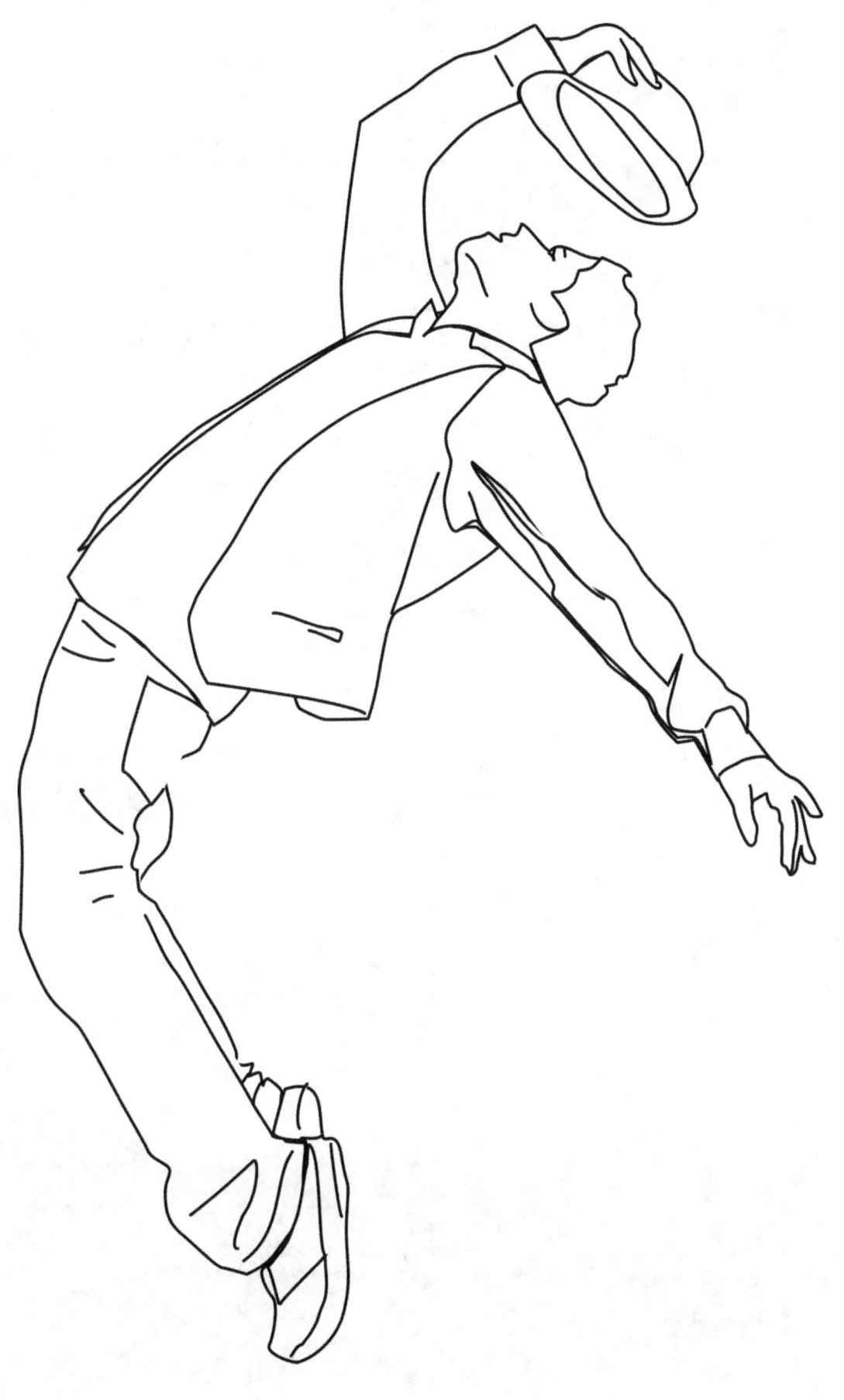

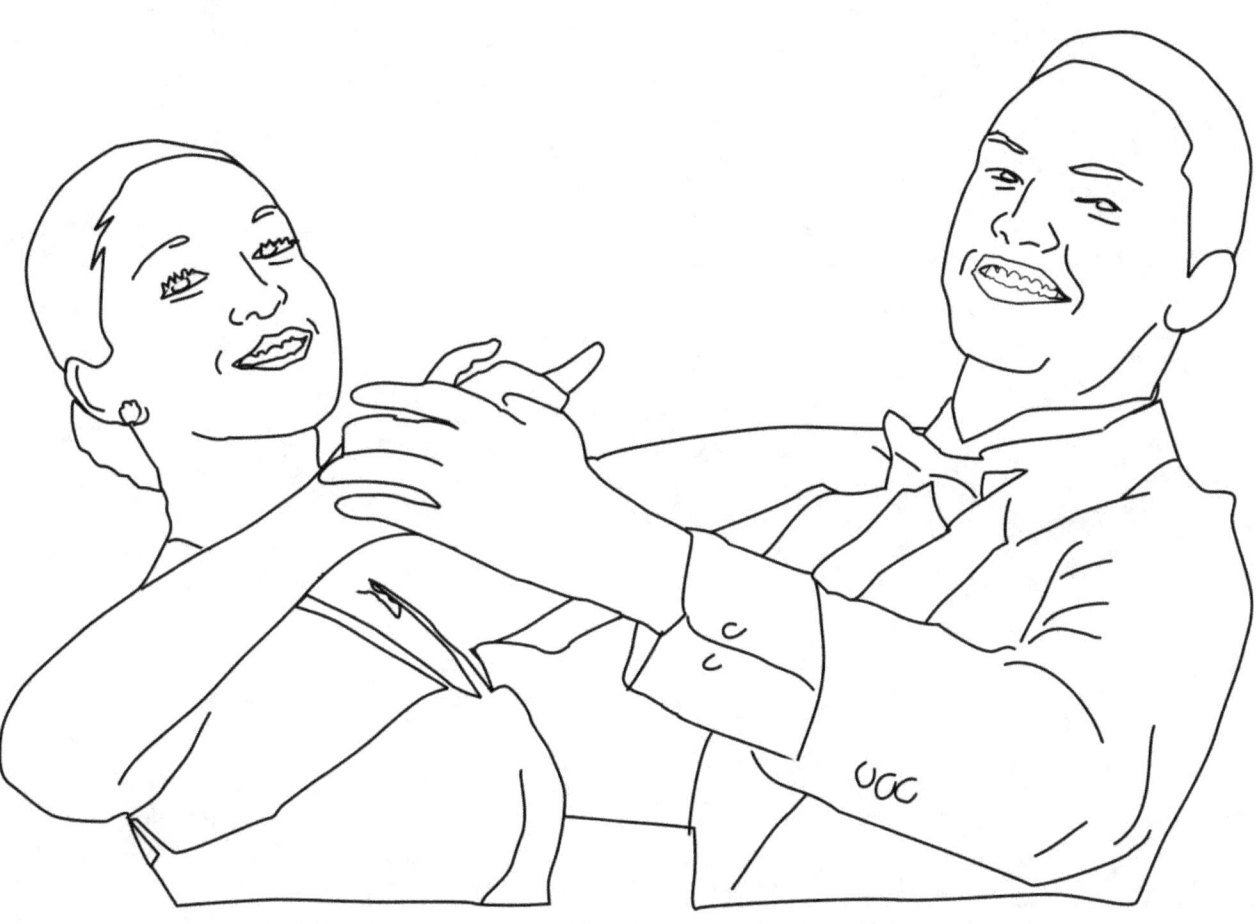

ARTIST

_____

NAME

_____

DATE

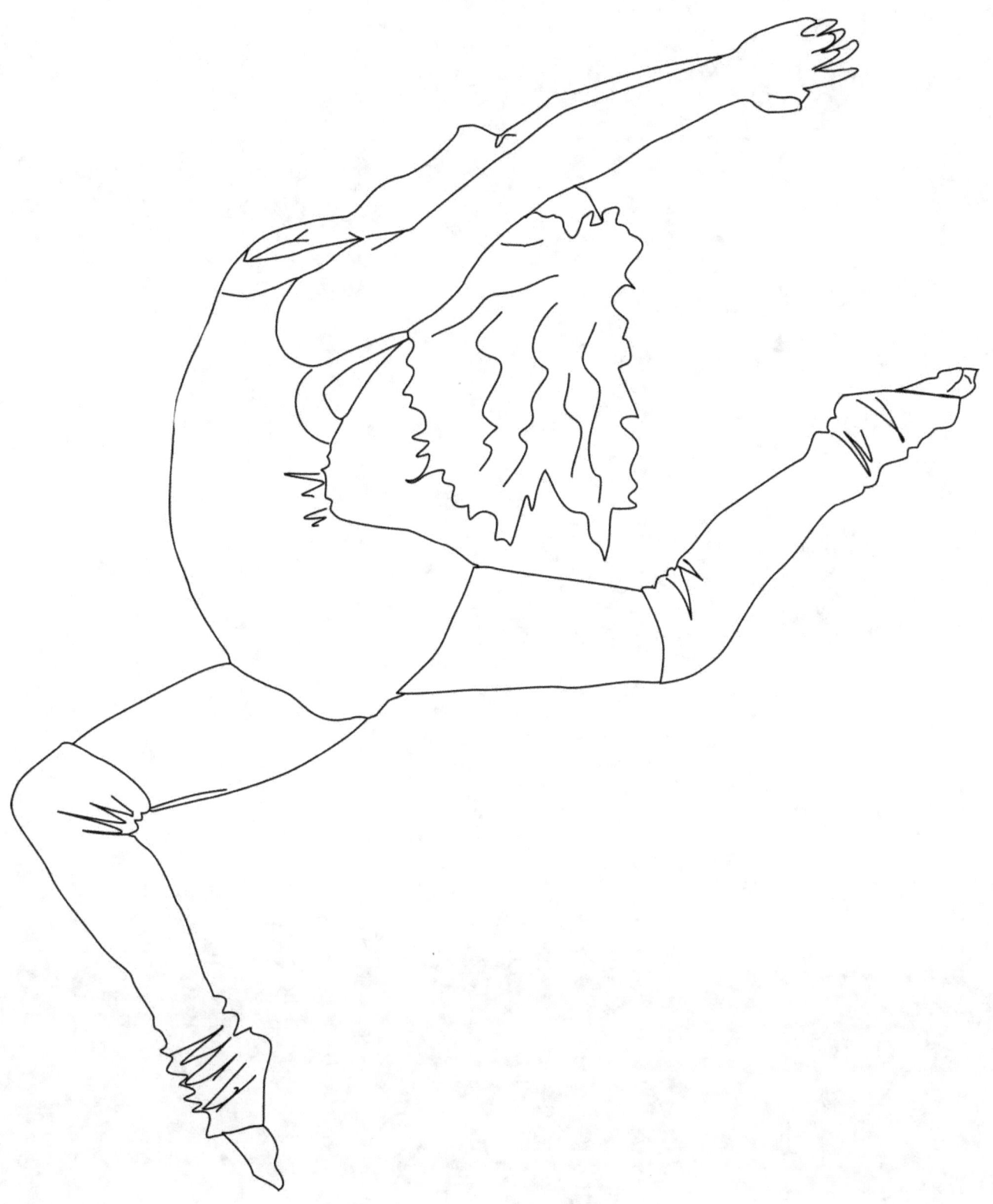

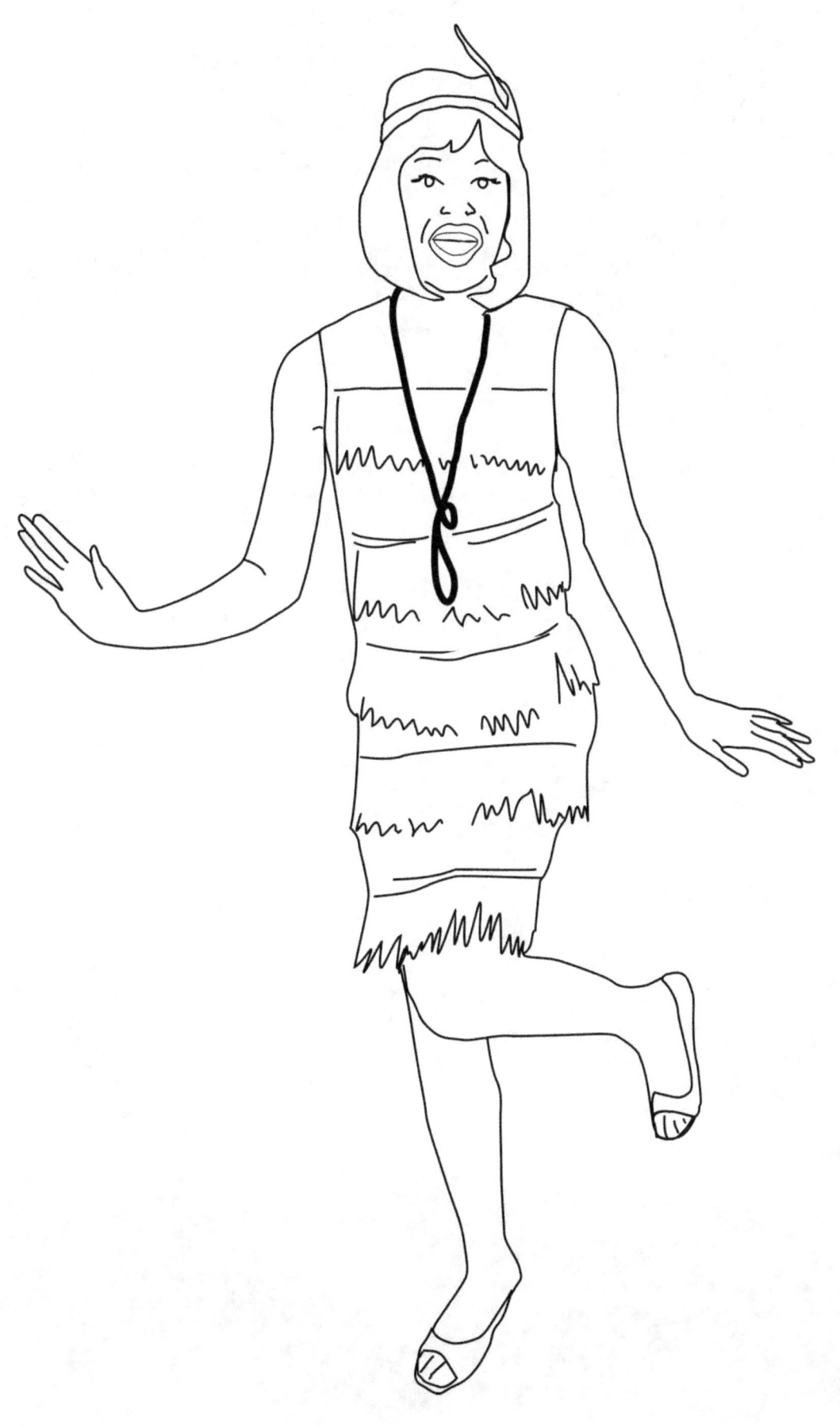

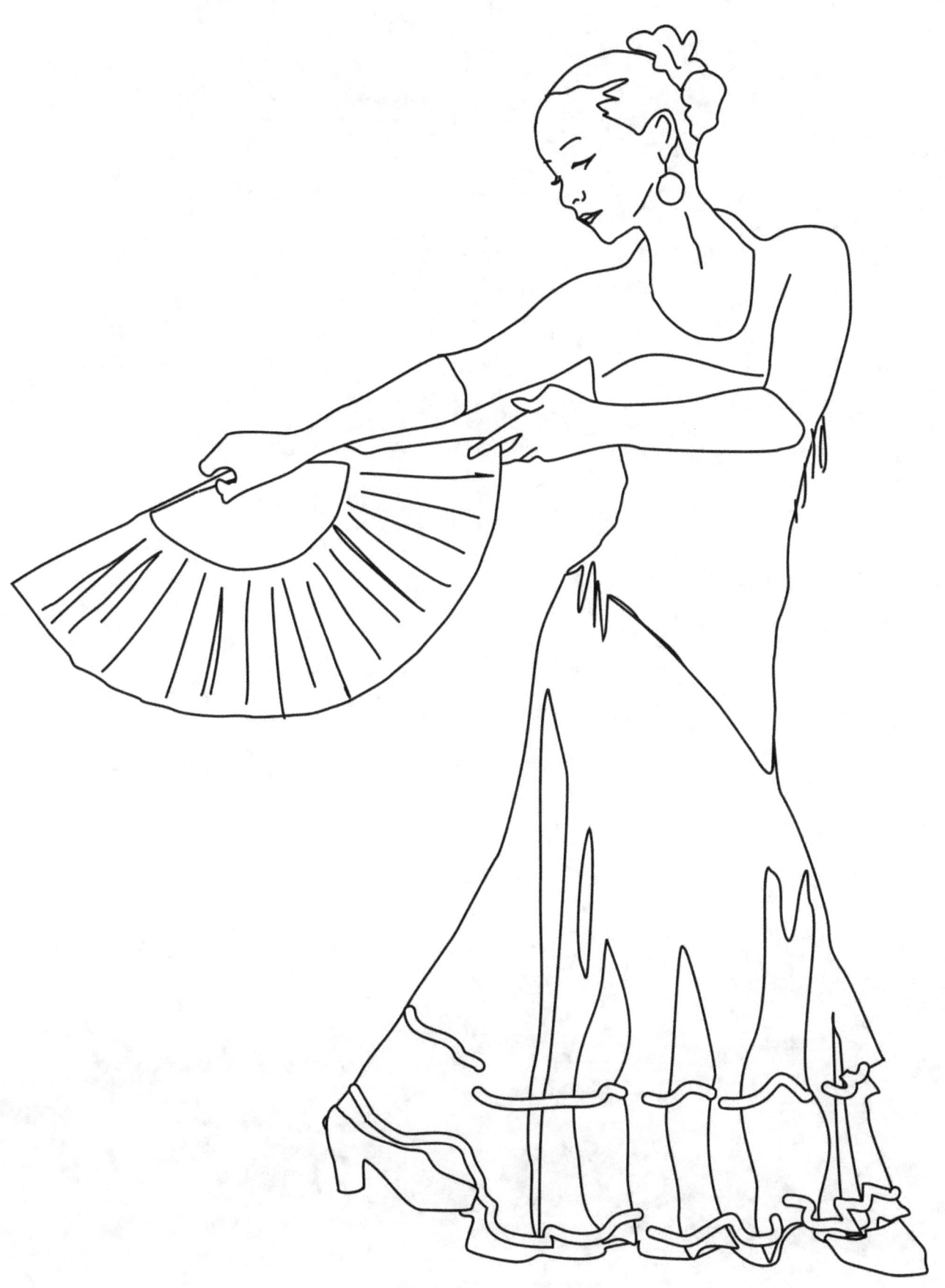

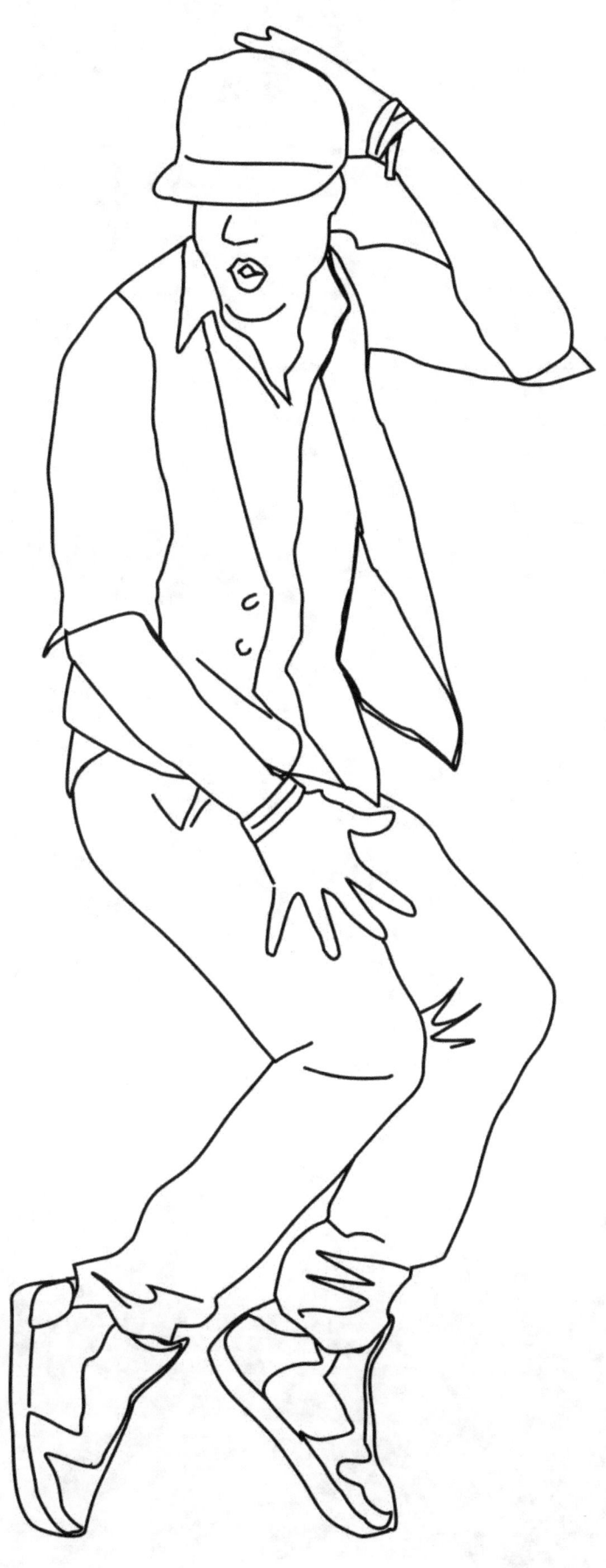

Artist Notes

Other Products

Please visit Jasmines author page for other coloring book titles.

www.amazon.com/author/jasminetaylor (https://goo.gl/AYQdxw)

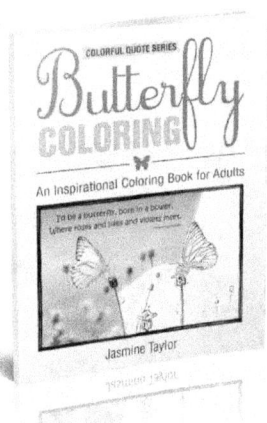

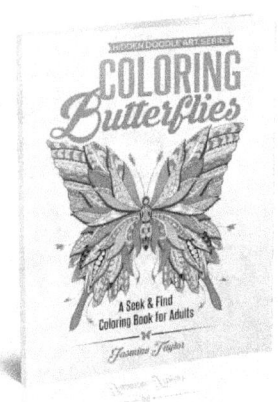

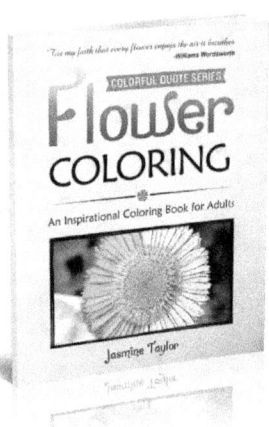

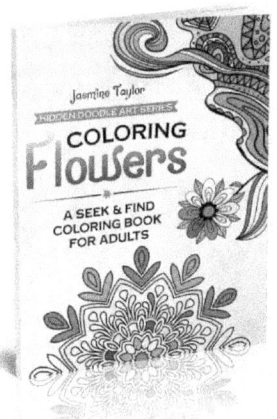

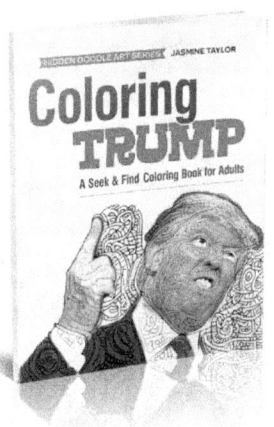

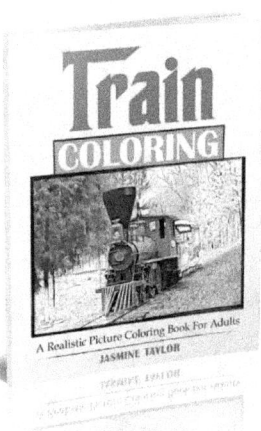

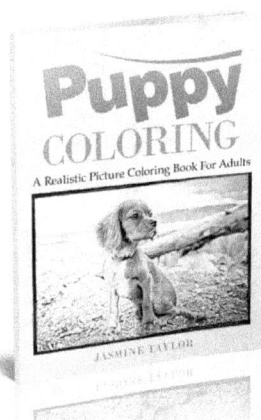

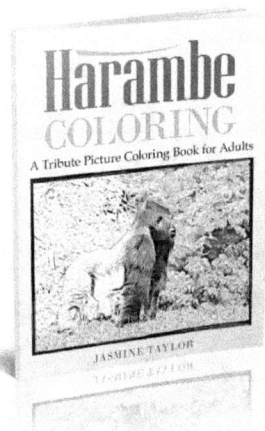

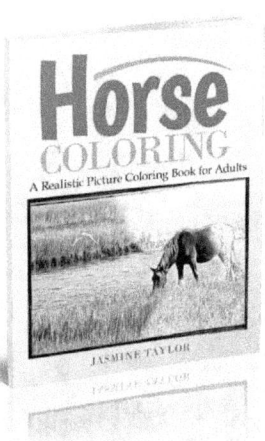

About the Author

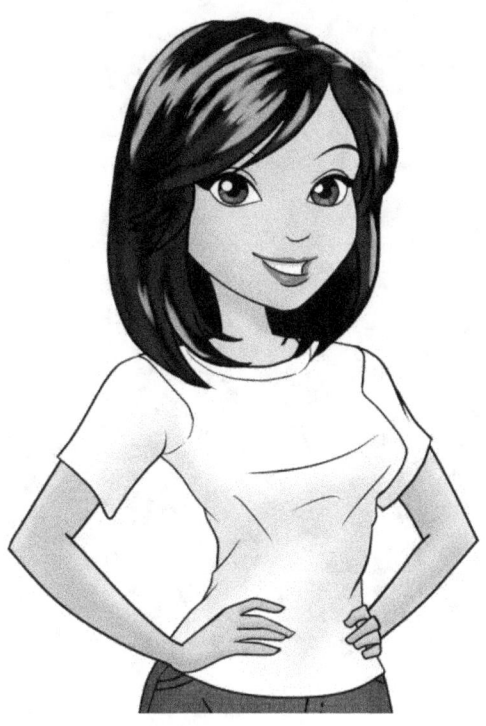

I'm passionate about art, coloring and creativity. My coloring books cover a variety of niches with varying styles and levels of difficulty from beginner to advance for all to enjoy. I'm really thrilled to offer my coloring books to you in the hope of inspiring your creative journey.

If you enjoyed this coloring book, please help others find and benefit as well by leaving a positive review on Amazon. Thank you very much and happy coloring!

Jasmine Taylor

www.ingramcontent.com/pod-product-compliance
Lightning Source LLC
Chambersburg PA
CBHW081308180526
45170CB00007B/2622